THE BEST
HOWLERS

THE BEST HOWLERS

By
CECIL HUNT

ERNEST BENN LIMITED
LONDON

First Published...................................*1928*
Eighth Impression *1932*
Second (revised) Edition...................*1949*

Published by Ernest Benn Limited
Bouverie House, Fleet Street, London
Printed by Hugh Paton and Sons Limited
Edinburgh

FOREWORD

IT is twenty years since this, my first collection of *Howlers*, was published. I am grateful to my publishers for reprinting it, with some revisions and additions, as *The Best Howlers*, so making it possible once more to meet the many requests for this book.

Since its original publication I have written many books, but *Howlers* remains one of the major satisfactions. It has brought—and continues to bring—grateful letters from all over the world. It is rewarding to an author to know that he has given laughter and encouragement to so many in isolation, in hospital, and in the rigours of active service conditions. The book has brought me many friends.

Lest any new readers should suspect me of a facile invention I would restate that I have invented nothing. Even if I were capable of creating howlers, there has been no need : the supply from readers is unabated, but none the less welcome.

I cannot claim that all these howlers are uncut gems. It is possible that some have been polished in the Common Room before transmission to me. But I can state that none known to be invented or improved has been consciously included.

To those who come fresh to the delights of howlers and suspect the authenticity of some of the more diverting ones, I would say that I have many thousands of these

howlers in the actual MS. in the original school exercise
books and examination papers. Many, equally diverting,
are, alas, unpublishable—such is the result, occasionally,
of juvenile innocence, ignorance and inconsequence. But
it would be a sad day for many if this fount of sparkling
humour ever failed.

CECIL HUNT.

SALFORD,
    CHIPPING NORTON,
        OXON.

1949.

CONTENTS

QUOTATION AND TRANSLATION

Letters in sloping type are in hysterics.

Infra dig.   In lodgings.

Ne plus ultra.   There is nothing beyond Ulster.

Pax in bello.   Freedom from indigestion.

Cæsar, secundum ventum nactus.   Cæsar, having got his second wind.

Du jambon cru.   What was thought to be ham.

Ni lui ni sa sœur sont Venus : Neither him nor his sister is a Venus.

Tertium quid.   A legal term for 6s. 8d.

Tout à fait.   All on the make.

Joie de vivre.   Whisky.

Ave Domine.   Lord, I am a bird.

LXXX.   Love and kisses.

Hors d'œuvre.   Out of work.

Honi soit qui mal y pense.   He may be honest who thinks badly.

Hors de combat.   War horse.

Coup de grâce.   Cup of grace.   A lawn mower.

Chevaux de frise.   Fried horse-flesh.

Cærulea puppis.   Sky terrier.

F.O.B.   Found on back.   Free of observation.   For ordinary business.   For old bachelors.   Following on behind.   Father of the Order of the Bath.

De mortuis nil nisi bonum.   In the dead there's nothing but bones.

Give the masculine of belle.   Stomach.

B.Sc. was interpreted as——Boy Scout, Bachelor's Scholarship, Borough School, and Brighton and South Coast.

P.S. was thought to mean——precious stones, plug cistern, police station, please stop, Piccadilly Circus, and Professor of Science.

O.B.E.   Observation balloon erector.

Un Espagnol de forte taille.   A spaniel with forty tails.

Combien d'oreilles un âne a-t-il ?   J'en ai deux.

Dido vento reditura secundo.   Dido will come again with her second wind.

e.g.   Egg sample.

" Each outcry of the wounded hair
  A fibre in the brain doth tare."

Put into French : I shall get on well if I go on as I am.   J'irai bien si je vaise sur comme je suis.

Translate : " Le Maître est tout noir et je n'ose pas rire."   The master is all black and I burst out laughing.

Pascebatque suas quisque senator oves.   Every senator used to live on his own eggs.

Translate : " Se dressait sur ses quatre pattes." Standing on his four pores.

Tenez ! dit Paolo Orso.   " Hold your polar bear," he said.

Il fit volte-face.   He made a horrid face.

" Des livres et journaux, protégés les jours de pluie par une toile tendue."   Books and newspapers forecasting the wet days by a tedious method.   Books and papers, delightful for rainy days after long toil.

Est-il parti, ma tante ?   Is there a party ? My Aunt !

Vere novo gelidus canis in montibus humor liquitur. Startling but true the cold hound was left on the mountains by way of a joke.

Pueri omnia animalium genera amabant.   The boys used to love all the sons-in-laws of the animals.

Brider l'âne par sa queue.   To brighten the year at its tail (this means Christmas).

Vespertinus circumgemuit ursus ovile.   The evening ear moaned round its egg.

Gallia omnis est divisa in partes tres.   All Gaul is quartered into three halves.

Cornigeri boves.   Corned beef.

Mes doux vers.   My two worms.

Festina lente.   The festival of Lent.

A quotation is an answer to a division sum.

The West Riding Regiment.   La cavalerie de l'ouest.

Place aux dames.   A ladies' waiting room.

Une maison bien orientée.   A beautifully decorated house.

Translations from the Latin : This predestined hour of disgrace arrived with groaning which was to make all things sadder by experiencing them than when they had forseen.

Do you hear how noisily the doors and the grove planted among the beautiful houses groans in the wind and how Jupiter freezes the snows placed in his serene godhead.

Catiline began to beg the senators not to believe that he was at all temeritous. He said that he derived his life and was sprung from adulescent family so that he had everything he could hope for.

Un paysan boiteux.   A countryman from the woods.

On verse le vin dans les verres.   They poured the wine to the worms.

Timbre-poste.   A wooden paling.

La levrette au cou de tourterelle.   The greyhound with the coo of a turtledove.

In Platonis libris omnibus Socrates exprimitur : Socrates was squeezed out of the omnibus by Plato's children.

Urit me Glyceræ nitor.   I am being burnt by nitro-glycerine.

Malitia non est jocus.   It is no joke to be in the Militia.

Pull down the blinds. Baissez les aveugles.

Très volontiers, répondit-il. Three volunteers responded.

Marcus amicus meus puellam amat. Marcus loves my friend's girl.

Trait d'union. Trade union.

D.V. Doctor of Vinity.

Mes souvenirs sont peu précis. My recollections are precious few.

Écrevisse. Girl typist.

Il avait à peine huit ans. He had a pain eight years.

Illi gemini erant liberi quattuor fere annorum. She had twins almost every four years.

Receptui canere. To sing at a reception.

Le lion se mit à rugir. The lion began to blush.

Il portait des souliers troués. He was wearing soldiers' trousers.

C'est bon à travailler, mais ce n'est pas bon de pas le faire. It is good to travel but it is not good to pay the fare.

The hind leg.   La jambe biche.

The money was left in his will.   L'argent fut gauche dans son volonté.

Je frappe, la sentinelle ouvre.   I knock the sentinel over.

Pueri, pauperum misereri discite.   Poor miserable boys, you must learn.

Cum grano salis.   Although with a corn, thou dancest.

Prenez garde que votre cheval ne prenne pas le mors entre les dents.   Take care that your horse does not die of toothache.

Canes domuum custodes sunt.   Canes are the guardians of the masters.

Des mouches d'une taille colossale.   Flies with colossal tails.

Il jeta un coup d'œil sur ses bagages.   He threw a cup of oil over his luggage.

A horse without a bridle.   Un cheval sans noces.

Rose, émue, répondit.   The rose emu laid another egg.

Quel âge avez-vous ?   Je suis treize ânes.

Il me reste peu de temps.   I have little time for resting.

Tu es un noble cœur.   You are a noble sister.

Les femmes suivaient leurs époux.   The women survived their husbands.

La reyne le veult.   The female fox wished for him.

Sub judice is the Bench on which the judges sit.

Will you be engaged this afternoon ?   Voulez-vous être fiancée cet après-midi ?

Il agitait les airs comme un ouragan.   It played beautiful tunes like an organ.

Pas de deux.   Father of twins.

K.G.   King of Greece.

M.D.   Mid Day.

P.M.   Post Mortem.

R.A.   Referee's Association.

F.R.G.S.   Fellow of the Royal General Surgeons.

Tête à tête : Having tea twice.

Britt. Omn : Rex : Fid : Def : Ind : Imp. Britain always rains, faithful, definite, indicative, imperfect.

R.I.P. Redmond's Imperial Parliament.

B.C. Before Christ. B.A. Before Adam.

Etc. It is a sign used to make believe you know more than you do.

Un grand Anglais avec son habituel sang froid. A tall Englishman with his usual adjectival cold.

C.O.D. Collector of debts. Cod Liver Oil Drink.

Ab ovo usque ad mala. It's up to the male to lay eggs.

Puellæ rosas pueri equos amant. The rosy girls love the boys on horseback.

Le canard ne saute pas. The duckling is not stewed.

Raison d'être. The right to live.

J'avais à cœur de vous tromper. I have a heart to trump you with.

Anno Domini means after death.

Adversum femur. A female adversary.

From the Pied Piper (No tuft on cheek, no beard on chin).   No turf on cheek, no bread on chin.

Corvi ovantes gutture.   Crows laying eggs in the gutter.

Incredibile est quantum civitas creverit.   It is incredible what a lot the citizen believes.

Praedamque ignara putabat.   And they, in their ignorance, took me for a beauty.

Venit servus tristi vultu.   The slave came with a sorrowful vulture.

Bouteilles du rhum.   Rheumatism boots.

Huile d'olivier.   Oily oblivion.

Il a un crêpe au chapeau.   He has crept into his hat.

Jeanne d'Arc porta une robe bien taillée.   Joan wore a tailor-made dress.

L'abbé était bien gras, car il aimait la bonne chère. The abbot was very fat, for he loved the dear nursemaid.

Cæsar transivit Alpes summa diligentia.   Cæsar crossed the Alps on the top of a diligence.

Feu la reine.   Fire on the queen.

Les oiseaux chantaient dans les arbres. The oysters were singing in the trees.

Translate " They have come " if " they " refers to a girls' school. Elles sont venuses.

Ce monsieur-là a perdu son amour-propre. The gentleman over there has lost his wife.

Felo de se. " Found drowned " — it is the French for " fell in the sea."

Leges utiles hominibus sunt. Legs are useful to men.

Emporté par la colère. Carried off by the collar.

Genæ puellæ formosæ sunt. Beautiful girls are cheeky.

J'ai hâté de l'embrasser. I hate to embrace her.

Fulminantis magna manus Iovis. The thundering big hand of Jove.

C.E.Z.M.S. (Church of England Zenana Mission Society). A high degree in music.

Columba alas albas habet. Columbus has an English atlas.

Derivation of " hypothesis." Hippo, horse ; thesis, placing. Putting something on a horse.

B.A.   Back ache.

Sotto voce.   In a drunken voice.

Stultissimus semper sua laudat.   A very foolish man always praises his own wife.

Translate " Lorsque viendra le temps des violettes. Nous ne trouverons pas leurs délicats squelettes," when " leurs " refers to the birds that have died during the winter.   When the violets come we shall not hear their delicate squeals.

Write in French " I saw some frogs in a stream." J'ai vu des crapauds dans un rissole.

Translate " Alphonse flânait tout le long de la journée dans la cour."   Alphonse remained all the journey in the pram.

Danaos, et dona ferentes.   The timid Danes fearing even their donahs.

MISCELLANY

Mushrooms always grow in damp places and so they look like umbrellas.

A refugee keeps order at a football match.

Rhubarb is a kind of celery gone bloodshot.

The Last Post is always sounded by the burglars of our School Spitoon.

The Prince of Wales uses a different title when he travels in the Congo.

The houses in old London could shake hands.

The stock exchange is where cattle and pigs are bought.

What qualifications are required for a special constable ? Any respectable man is illegible.

In the United States people are put to death by elocution.

All teachers at —— Council School are certified.

Parsimony is money left by your father.

A schoolmaster leads a sedimentary life.

Crematorium.   French for a dairy.

A prospectus is a man who finds gold.

A railway station is a place where we wait for trains.

Excuse for absence.   I am sorry I am unable to attend school, but yesterday I fell and cut my knee on a piece of glass and to-day I have a pane in my leg.

In some buses they have smoking aloud.

Michael Angelo painted the selling of the cistern chapel.

The Court of Chancery is so-called because it takes care of property when there is no chance of the owner turning up.

The pineapple is the fruit of the pine tree.

A glazier is a man who runs down mountains.

The shop windows looked very gay; lump sugar, granulated, and castor were arranged in different coloured bowls according to their sex.

He did not give a name to this picture, but called it " A unanimous picture of an old lady."

Peat is made out of moses.

There was the sea and that was another handy cup.

The feast was held for two days and no children were aloud.

The Plimsoll line is used on ships to tell the climate and the deapth of water where the ship is.

Hiatus : breath that wants seeing to.

Every morning in summer the son came shining in at my window.

Essay on Summer.   In the meadows you can see snowdrops and daffodils and growing on the hedges are roses and honeysuckle and the people gather blackberries.

He sailed away in his ship and got his destiny safe.

It was moonlight and the air was soft and putrid.

Before being captain of his ship he had worked as an amiable seaman.

The dodo is a bird that is nearly decent.

Flax is really wheat which is afterwards made into bread.

As the creator cools it hardens.

All the crew were taken into custardy.

Marconi is used to make delicious puddings.

An undergraduate is a person not up to the mark. A lower class of board school.

Nets are holes surrounded by pieces of string.

Newspapers are useful for reporting calamities such as deaths, marriages, etc.

Bass is a beverage made from a fish of that name.

The opposite of evergreen is nevergreen.

Barbarians are things put into bicycles to make them run smoothly.

If it is noon and the sun is straight above you, you are north.

If anyone should faint in church put her head between the knees of the nearest medical man.

Our seamen are cheerful, happy, and brave, for they know nothing of things going to happen to them in the future.

A child whose name was preceded by " van " was asked if her father was Dutch. " No, but my descendants were Dutch " was the delightful reply.

The Navy, although very large and clever, needs the lifeboat to keep a watch over it.

The lifeboat is wonderfully constructed so that it can carry more than it can hold.

The Lifeboat service is to save lives, if it did not people would get scarce.

Skyscrapers are large telescopes.

A skyscraper is an over-trimmed hat.

The Crystal Palace is where the King and Queen reign.

Les Invalides. Women that can't do anything at all.

Eiffel Tower is a pudding.

Cripps is a modern prophet who seems more interested in loss.

A vegetable cell is a place very dark and gloomy where greengrocers who sell bad vegetables go.

What is the Yellow Peril? It is the name sometimes given to the Girl of America.

It is the sickness taken by English or European colonists when they settle in Africa, and in all countries where gold dust is found. It has been the death of hundreds who get gold dust in their lungs.

What are duties of a lunacy commissioner? He has to see that people are insane enough to enter a lunatic asylum. He is the Commander of a lunatic.

Sailors do not like the sea when it is rough because it is very dangerous, and then many lives have been lost and few of them found again.

What are the duties of an auditor? A man who calls out in the House of Commons.

He is the chief hearer in a Court of Justice.

One whose work is to keep silence or order during any notable event open to the public.

What is Excise? A mode or manner by which authorities extortion money from inhabitants for the King to pay the National Debt.

A duty which must be performed by a man who undertakes the job.

It is good for us to have excise in the open air, as the air vibrates through our muscells.

The duty paid on goods in possession of ships' passenger, if the goods are new.

A pilot is a promoted sailor to do all the work on deck. His duties are to see that every ship that comes into port is perfectly clean, and has brought no disease.

A pilot is a sea-robber, who robs every ship he comes in contact with.

A grass widow is the wife of a dead vegetarian.

A close time is when the Houses of Parliament are not sitting.

A close time is when all the public houses close their doors to drink customers.

Etiquette is the noise you make when you sneeze.

Etiquette teaches us how to be polite without trying to remember to be.

Psyche was a black boxer who fought Carpentier.

What is an herbaceous border?   One who boards all the week and goes home on Saturdays and Sundays.

Policemen are called " peelers " because Sir Robert Peel was the first policeman.

Why does a kettle sing?   Because if it didn't we could not tell when the kettle was boiling.

A down bed is a bed on the floor.

Petroleum is what you cover floors with.

A fort is a place to put men in, a fortress is a place to put women in.

The jockey lost two of his teeth when his horse fell, and had to be destroyed.

" Bring out your dead " is what the judges said when a prisoner was brought for trial from the cells.

Writing of the school's old boys in an essay on the war : Those that did not go to the war married, but the stronger ones got up a Rugby football team.

What is a bead ?   A bede is a very old man, known as a venerable bede or sometimes as Adam Bede.

The flannelette peril means petticoat government.

A convoy is a collection of partridges.

A lock-out is a man who comes home too late.

With a view to comparing old - time means of transport with present facilities a class was invited to write an imaginary dialogue between a cab-horse and an aeroplane.   This is how a Bristol boy opened :— Horse : " What is that blasted thing up in the air ? "

The City of Westminster is remarkable for the quantity of laws and things that get past.

All rent, rates, and taxes are given to the King, for the purpose of many different things, such as the dustmen, the lamps at night, and the workhouses. Generally the rent is collected by the landlord and given to the county council and then paid to the King.

Hall Caine is the maker of cricket bats (all cane).

Dust is mud with the juice squeezed out.

Snoring is letting off sleep.

Terra cotta is stuff squeezed out of a little insect and used to turn puddings red.

A fan is a thing you brush the warm off with.

The Boat Race is rowed from Putney to Moorgate.

A barrister is a thing which is put up in the street to keep the crowds back.

Mungo Park was discovered by the famous explorer, David Livingstone. Stock and agriculture are the chief industries of Mungo Park.

In the eighteenth century travelling was very romantic, most of the high roads were only bridal paths.

A Trade Union is a place to which a workman goes when he gets the sack.

London Matriculation is what you must do to get a job.

Cromlechs are fibrous substances found in Scotland, out of which a sort of incombustible cloth is manufactured.

The round towers are tall towers built in memory of the dead, but for what purpose is not known.

What is dusk? Little bits of stuff that fly about in the air.

To be called to the Bar is to be treated to a drink.

What is the correct name for a five-shilling piece? A bob.

The Greenwich Meridian is the largest telescope in Greenwich Observatory.

A welsher is a native of Wales.

A bibulous man is one who frequently quotes from the Scriptures.

Extracts from answers describing how London is supplied with water, from a London County junior scholarship examination. Water is put into large tanks and filleted. Water is stored in a system and released by a tape. These pipes lead to what we call a viceroy; this viceroy is filled with water.

A ghost is an invisible object which cannot be seen in the daytime but only at night.

Man power. Someone or something that is very strong. When a man has much more strength than a woman.

The White Feather. A Feather that is white in colour as a white Leg Horn's is.

One of the uses of leaves to a plant is expiration. This goes on day and night, same as in human beings.

Extracts from essays following a lecture on work among the deaf.

We shall get Deff and Dum when we get our teeth out.

We pay money to you to go and give the deaf and dumb a feed of cake.

If you make a shock you will be deaf and dumb.

An ear tube is a funny thing with electricity in the middle and something the other end for the person to hear with that you listen to.

An epitaph is a horse with the head of a man.

A hostage is a lady who entertains visitors.

Cheese is butter gone bad.

The embalmed body of an Egyptian is called a dummy.

A republican is a sinner mentioned in the Bible.

A knave is a man which works on the tramlines.

A parsimonious boy is a boy who wants to be a parson.

Ladies wear oyster feathers in their hats.

A widow is a wife without a man.

The streets of London are often pinned down by lamp-posts.

Many new faces toed the line at our school walking match.

The leek is what St David ate when he preached in Wales.

There is a man who watches the Highlands at night, he is called the Black Watch.

" Alias " was a good man mentioned in the Bible.

Glaziers are common, they move about one foot per day in Switzerland.

A certain type of bag is named after a great statesman, who was he ?   Lord Oxford.

Strathspey.   A battle with spades.
An empty whiskey bottle.

Tarzan is a short name for the American flag. It's full name is Tarzan Stripes.

BIBLICAL

The first book in the Bible is Guinessis.

Christians are only allowed one wife. This is called monotony.

The Clapham Sect live in Clapham unction.

Infants' department, singing morning hymn. "We can sing full though we be!" (Weak and sinful though we be.)

Acrimony (sometimes called holy) is another name for marriage.

Evolution is what Darwin did, Revolution is a kind of government abroad, Devolution has something to do with Satan.

St Bartholomew's Day is noted for the massacre of the Hottentots.

Jacob went in search of the Golden Fleece.

"Seeking a bible reputation even in the canon's mouth."

An epistle is the wife of an apostle.

The Pharisees were people who liked to show off their goodness by praying in synonyms.

Abraham, after the sacrifice of Isaac, called the place Rio Janeiro.

A little girl's version of the parable of the lost sheep : " The shepherd counted his sheep 99 there were again 99 I must look for that one. Down in a pit among some ferns he heard a bleat he got it and took it home and gave it some hot grass."

Zacharias was burning insects when he saw an angel.

A deacon is the lowest form of christian.

Esau was a man who wrote fables and sold his copyright for a mess of potash.

Jacob was a patriarch who brought up his twelve to be patriarchs, but they did not take to it. Jacob didn't eat much, as a rule, except when there was a famine in the land.

Abraham was chiefly noted for his bosom.

What is an occasional office (dealing with the Prayer Book) ? An occasional office is one that is not used regularly, such as the consecration of a cemetery or the Churching of a Bishop.

Chaplets are small places of worship.

Martin Luther was nailed to the church door at Wittenburg for selling papal indulgences.

The Philistines are islands in the Pacific.

What do you know of Solomon? He was very fond of animals because he had three hundred porcupines.

John Wesley was a great sea captain. He beat the Dutch at Waterloo and by degrees rose to be Duke of Wellington. He was buried near Nelson in the Poet's Corner at Westminster Abbey.

Noah was the man who danced before the ark, but he first sent the bird away.

The locusts were the chief plague. They ate all the first-born.

The Septuagint was a committee of 700 men elected to revise the poems of Homer.

Solomon had 300 wives and 700 cucumbers.

The Primate is the wife of the Prime Minister.

The spies brought a report of the city of Jerico and said the land was flowing with milk and honey, and brought a big bunch of grapes to prove it.

And some fell on stony ground and the fowls of the air sprang up and choked them.

Abraham was a bellowing sheep. (? Bedouin sheik.)

Faith is that quality by which we believe what we should otherwise think was false.

Salome was a very wicked woman who wore very few clothes and took them all off when she danced before Harrods.

A lie is an abomination unto the Lord, but a very present help in trouble.

St Alban died a mitre.

St Alban was the first British martha.

When Moses died, Joshua was his predecessor.

Samuel asked what the bleating of sheep and the braying of oxen was about.

As Isaac grew up he always domineered, so the only thing to do was to turn him into the dessert.

Saul was commanded to kill everybody. This he did in a half-hearted fashion as he nailed the King to a tree.

The Decalogue is a low-necked frock.

Abraham was the first plague. He is still remembered actively.

My mother is a famous church-woman. She washes up the Sunday School teas.

Solomon in all his glory was not a rabbit like one of these.

The people of Athens wouldn't believe what Paul said much. Edinburgh is like Athens.

El Dorado. King Saul's sheep man.

Remember that thou keep holy the Sabbath Day, six days shalt thou labour and do no work.

Explain what is meant by bearing false witness against one's neighbour. It was when nobody did nothing, and somebody went and told of it.

What did the Israelites do when they came out of the Red Sea? They dried themselves.

The Israelites made a golden calf because they hadn't got enough gold to make a cow.

A certain man drew his bow at a venture, but missed the venture and hit Ahab.

An essay on the flight of the Jews from Egypt. And they received manna in their dessert.

During the Reformation every clergyman was compelled to receive thirty nine articles.

Explain the meaning of bishop, priest, and deacon. I never saw a bishop so I don't know. A priest is a man in the Old Testament. A deacon is a thing you pile on the top of a hill and set fire to it.

Who came first out of the Ark? I don't know, but Noah came fourth.

Aaron was a good man, who helped Moses with his conjuring tricks.

What did Moses do for a living while he was staying with Jethro? He married one of his daughters.

What is the outward and visible sign or form in Baptism? The baby.

Define a graven image. The thing put in the grave when they are buried.

And having our loins girt about with the helmet of salvation.

Sodom and Gomorrah are two famous volcanoes in Europe.

A Protestant is any one who is not a Catholic. Roman Catholics believe what the Pope speaks, but Protestants can believe what they like.

The Papal Bull is the animal kept at the Vatican to feed the Pope's children.

What did St. Paul do when he re-visited his churches ?   A Girl Guide's answer : On his first visit he enrolled many Christians, and on his second he appointed patrol leaders.

Jacob had a brother called Aseesaw.

Sepulchre :   derived from " se " negative and " pulcher " fair.   The place where beauty fades.

A synagogue is something like a church.   A place where sinners worship.

A monastery is a place where they make money.

An idolator is a very idle person.

Noah's wife was Joan of Arc.

A parable is a heavenly story with no earthly meaning.

A Bishop without a diocese is called a suffragist.

Stipend.   When you are in a room full of smoke you are stipend.
What a parson preaches his sermon on.

Rector.   Something worked by electricity.
Something in parts to be put together.

Jethro was the son of Moses.

A passover is a man who goes from bad to worse, like Judas Iscariot.

A monastery is a very big statue like those you see in London like the monastery of great sailors like Nelson whose monastery is still standing.

Moses was single but he was certainly a father in the dessert.

The rhythem of the Bible is usually unrhyming Diameters.

And he said : " What shall I do to inherit internal life ? "

Gross darkness is a kind of religious darkness, one hundred and forty-four times as dark as ordinary dark.

HISTORY AND POLITICS

The British Constitution is a sound one, but on account of its insolent position it suffers from fogs.

Charles I was going to marry the Infanta of Spain. He went to see her, and Shakespeare says he never smiled again.

William the Conqueror was thrown from his horse and wounded in the feudal system and died of it.

The Minister of War is the clergyman who preaches to the soldiers in the barracks.

Charles II told the people they could get drunk and gamble and do what they liked. This was called the Restoration.

The King was not to order taxis without the consent of Parliament.

Henry VIII was very fat, besides being a Non-conformist.

Henry VIII would not allow Peter Spence to go to Rome.

John Bright was famous for an incurable disease.

Henry the First's son, William, was drowned in the White Ship, and never smiled again.

Lambert Simnel was defeated at Stoke and sent to roast in the King's kitchen.

Joan of Arc lived in the French Revolution, and one day she fell into the arms of the English and got burnt.

When a drunken man sees what a fool he has been and is going to turn over a new leaf he is called a reformer. John Wycliff was a reformer.

Simon de Montford formed what was known as the Mad Parliament. It is something the same as it is at the present time.

The Gordian Knot was untied by Lord Kitchener when he took Khartoum and cleared up the tangle into which we had got over General Gordon.

Joan of Arc was the daughter of a pheasant.

Queen Elizabeth had a great sporting spirit and she was weaned from her man o' war with difficulty.

When Napoleon decided to invade England he gathered together all the flat bottomed bargees.

The people of Vennas used to call their king a dog, but they did not prernounce it the same.

The New Forest was made by William II as a place to keep his dear in, and if any men came after his dear and the king heard about it he had their eyes put out.

Julius Cæsar was renowned for his great strength. He threw a bridge across the Rhine.

Another large building in Egypt is Cleopatra's Needle. It is covered with Roman writing which is still audible though it has been on for many hundreds of years.

They gave the Duke of Wellington a lovely funeral. It took six men to carry the beer.

Once or twice the muskets of the soldiers inside the wooden horse rattled against the side of the horse.

Guy's Hospital was built to commemorate the Gunpowder Plot.

Taxes are things what people won't pay. They are used to keep the roads nice.

Queen Elizabeth was called the Virgil Queen because she knew Latin.

Queen Elizabeth never marrid, she had a peaceful reign.

King John ground the people down under heavy taxis.

A sinecure is a job with a portfolio and pay and no work. In a sense Henry VIII was a sinecure king.

The Socialists don't believe in hereditary titles; they make peers of those who don't work.

Richard II was murdered in Pontefract Castle, but his fate is unknown.

A Limited Monarchy is a government by a monarch, who, in case of a bankruptcy, would not be entirely responsible for the National Debt. You have the same thing in private life with a Limited Liability Company.

Charles II refused to allow his subjects to partition him, but the Bill of Rights gave them permission to do so.

William ordered his archers to shoot at the thickest part of the English, so they shot upwards so that the arrows might fall on the Englishmen's heads.

Chequers is a public house near Wales.

A lot of money is wasted every year on the Army and Navy because they are so costive.

Preparations are things done in advance of something else, such as packing your bag or cleaning your teeth before retiring.

William the Conquer surrounded the Isle of Ely with his feet.

The Barons all had strong livered attendants and it was these the king was rightly frightened of.

Columbus discovered America, and was the first man.

Bruce was a brave general, and fought like a spider.

My favourite character in English history is Henry VIII because he had eight wives and killed them all.

The cause of the Peasant's Revolt was that a shilling poultice should be put on everybody over sixteen.

Edward III would have been King of France if his mother had been a man.

The Domesday Book was a book in which all about estates was written down so as to see about taxis. A book signifying that each man should have seven feet of land for a grave. Domesday Book is another name for Paradise Lost.

Alexander the Great was born in the absence of his parents.

The chief clause in Magna Carta was that no free man should be put to death or imprisoned without his own consent.

The Feudal System lies between the Humber and the Thames.

What do you know of Dryden and Buckingham? Dryden and Buckingham were at first friends, but soon after became contemporaries.

Austerity is a very ancient religion but nowadays even politicians believe it.

The Partition of Poland was a wall built to keep the Germans out of Russia.

Julius Cæsar was murdered in the Cenotaph.

Henry VIII had the Prayer Book put into English to spite the Pope, who wanted to marry Catherine of Arragon.

William III on his way to Hampton Court, tumbled over a mole and broke his collarbone—which was fatal to a man of his constituency.

Under Henry VIII the Bible was translated into Latin by Titus Oates, whom the King ordered to be chained up in church for greater security.

Prince Henry was drowned in the wash. The story goes that he never smiled again.

The Normans used to put mokes round their castles to protect them from attack.

Henry I died from a surfeit of palfreys.

Mary, Queen of Scots, went to France and married the Dauphin. A year later the Dauphin died.

At the battle of Crecy the English mowed down the French with their hoes and barrows.

Describing the incident of Sir Walter Raleigh laying down his cloak, a lad wrote : " Her Majesty remarked to Sir Walter, ' I am afraid I have spoiled your cloak,' to which the gallant knight replied, ' Dieu et mon droit,' which means, ' My God, and you're right ! ' "

Now Henry had an abbess on his knee, which made walking difficult.

Queen Elizabeth rode through Coventry with nothing on, and Raleigh offered her his cloak.

In 1620 the Pilgrims crossed the ocean, which is known as the Pilgrim's Progress.

Joan of Arc was Noah's sister.

Queen Elizabeth was the last of the Roses, and, fearing that Mary, Queen of Scots, would marry her husband, Sir Walter Raleigh, she beheaded her, and in remorse sent Raleigh to discover the United States. When he returned without doing so he was executed by Elizabeth's son, James I, after gaining time to write his long and varied biography in the Tower.

Mr Atlee is decisively an imminent politician.

Henry VIII was really a musician at heart so he had many wives to call the tune. He left evidence of his art.

Sir Stafford Cripps is a lawyer who has been in labour ever since he entered politics.

Cæsar extinguished himself on the battlefields of Gaul.

One of Drake's most famous exploits was singing the King of Spain's beard.

The Lollards' aim was to abolish churches altogether and in the churches that were left to have nothing unnecessary.

Prisons in the Norman period were not like ours; they were dull and dreary.

The Britons were in a blight with having no warriors and two foes.

Henry V spent all his time with low-down thieves and made life a pleasure.

The New Forest in William the First's reign was out of bounds for all villagers.

The battle of Sluys was fought at sea. It was one of those battles in which the bowmen did better work than the cavalry.

Spivs are people who work in ways the Government hasn't thought of.

Members of Parliament are mostly business men. This is necessary, otherwise they wouldn't earn a living.

The Romans have left tasselled pavements.

The Scotch hatted the English.

By a trick the Persians were enjuiced to attack.

When the Black Prince died it was called the Black Death.

What is a Mayor ? A man chosen to be head of the Town Council and to grant holidays to the schools for one year.

A lockout is like a strike only it lasts longer.

The principal thing which was left behind by the Egyptians was their bones.

Ridley and Lattimer were scented to death.

On one side of a penny is the King's head, on the other a young lady riding a bicycle ; they call her Ruby Tanyer.

Rome wasn't built in a day is an old saying now adopted as the motto of the building industry.

D

The Lollards were burnt at the steak.

Cæsar was soon given news of the approach of Cleopatra's burnished poop as it was very conspicuous in the distance.

Oliver Cromwell's home policy was that of being a good husband and a kind father. His foreign policy was to walk abroad in a big slouch hat and a very large red nose.

The attempts at colonisation in Elizabeth's reign were that Raleigh brought smoking into England and had a bucket of cold water thrown on him, and Drake discovered potatoes round the world and planted them in Lancashire.

The Chartists demanded Universal Suffering and Triangular Parliaments.

The Poll Tax was to be paid by everybody who had a head.

Wolsey's fate is attributed to his having shot at the Pope.   (Text book : " Aimed at the Papacy.")

A crow at the mast-head of a French ship fired twice at Nelson and then killed him.

By the Statute of Mortmain clergymen were not allowed to receive land from people who died without the King's consent or paying a tax.

The Act of Uniformity provided that every one must take an oath of Passive Resistance.

Wycliffe's great work was the translation of the Bible into Middle English, because he thought the people would be more likely to understand the English spoken in the Midlands.

Who is Anthony Eden ?   A dirty port in Suez, mostly used for coaling.

The patience of Job is another name for the Civil Service.

Why does true English history begin with the reign of Henry VII ?   Because up to this time it was all lies.

When great men die they leave their memorandums in Westminster Abbey.

Henry VIII was brave, corpulent and cruel, he was frequently married to a widow, had an ulcer on his leg and great decision of character.

The Prodigal Fathers sailed for the New World in 1620.

The provisions of Oxford were wheat, sheep, eggs, etc.

Mention the illegal acts of James II.   The birth of a son.

The Navigation Act prohibited any goods from being exported except to the country where they were manufactured.

Simon de Montfort's father was a Crusader, and from him he inherited religiousness, which was very useful to him afterwards when he became Archbishop of Canterbury.

Sir Thomas More is a famous man who has just been carbonised by the Roman Catholics.

At the Field of the Cloth of Gold Henry VIII wore a long train, composed of many followers.

By the Petition of Rights courting soldiers were not allowed in private houses.

Another name for the Bloody Statute was Queen Mary. She was called that because she would not speak.

Political economy is the science which teaches us to get the greatest benefit with the least possible amount of honest labour.

Where are the Kings of England crowned ?   On their heads.

Where was Magna Carta signed ?   At the bottom.

Sir Robert Peel founded the police force. He also found a grave in Westminster Abbey.

Guerilla warfare means up to their monkey tricks.

The Budget is a list of grievances secretly presented to the Prime Minister to rectify the unemployed.

What is the Soviet?   The Soviet is what the middle-classes call their napkin.

The Romans drove Pixies over Hadrian's Wall.

What are the Wee Frees?   A band of men like Socialists.   Supporters of the Free State.   The tenants of small houses who pay no rent.   We Frees when we are cold.

The Navy is sometimes called the Senile Service.

At the battle of Crecy the soldiers found a Ford motor van, by which they crossed the river.   (Due to unexplained use of the word " ford " by teacher.)

Pompeii was destroyed by an overflow of saliva from the Vatican.

The French Revolution was won violently, not by " freedom slowly broadening down from President to President," as Tennyson wrote.

In Henry VII's reign even the most turbulent barons received a cheque from the king.

Antony and Bismark are two of the metals.

Cæsar swam the Rubicon because his boats were all burnt.

By the Constitutions of Clarendon no son of a villian was to become a commercial without the king's permission.   (Text book reading : " to take orders.")

At the coronation of Henry III when the little king had been crowned all his barons stood round and swore at him.

The Mad Parliament was so called because it rejected the Home Rule Bill.

Hannibal is a well-known music writer.

The conquest of Ireland began in 1170 and is still going on.

Of Queen Mary of Scotland.   She was wilful as a girl and cruel as a woman ; but what can you expect from a person who had five step-mothers ?

The Wars of the Roses killed a lot of the important knights and they never got another start.

Elizabeth had a better claim to the throne than Mary for she had possession nine-tenths of the throne by law.

During the interdict in John's reign, births, marriages and deaths were not allowed to take place.

Joan of Arc won her chief battle because the enemy's wind came across to her. As soon as that happened she knew God was on her side.

The King was crowned in the Crystal Palace with his sepulchre in his hand.

Clive had some ships, their names were the Pelican and a few more. One time when there was a war going on with Spain Clive and a few other men were having a game of bowels, and the Spaniards were coming near . . .

The Cabal was a ministry to place wireless telegraphy.

Queen Mary had all the Protestants put under the steak.

Henry VIII married Amberlim.

The Invisible Armada was so called because you couldn't see it.

Henry VIII was very pious, and he had a hymn book chained up in every church.

What do you know of Henry VIII ? I can't answer that as we are not doing the Old Testament now.

Sir Philip Sidney is famous for retreating with a water bottle when the wrong dispatches were received. He also had poetic gifts and a shinning sense of humour.

Catherine of Arragon was pushed off the throne by Anne Boleyn.

Thomas à Becket was standing on the alter when four nights came and killed him.

A Welsh prince was born to please Wales.

The feudal system was that a large tin was put over the fire so that it would go out at seven o'clock.

Parliament was a house where men sat and disgusted bills.

Dunstan was a good man, but he did not like studying at Eton, so he left and went into a convent, and soon after became Archbishop of Glastonbury.

Henry VIII was a broad-shouldered man.　　Mary was a narrow-minded woman.

The Provisions of Oxford were that the King should stop at home and provide people.

William the Conqueror was the first of the Mormons.

The names of the five members were Pym and four others.

In the Five Mile Act no one who was a Catholic was allowed to go within five miles of anywhere ; nor might he be a teacher when he got there.

James I had a monopoly on all herrings brought to London. Soon after he died.

Until Ralegh brought tobacco back, Elizabeth regarded him as one of her nights.

Cassandra was a Trojan profiteer.

Who would reign if the King died ?　The Queen. And if there was no Queen living ?　The knave.

The battle of Trafalgar Square was fought in London against the Spaniards. One of those who fell in this battle was Nelson.

London was spoilt by the great fire. It is much worse now than it used to be.

The Three Estates of the Realm are Windsor, Sandringham, and Balmoral.

Martin Luther did not die a natural death, he was excommunicated by a bull.

Phillippa was a brave queen ; she married Edward I.

The death of Julius Cæsar was foretold by a shower of metaphors.

The great Duke of Malborough was a man of exceedingly fine character, omitting his vices, which were many.

What do you mean by Habeas Corpus ? A treatise on the circulation of the body.

Who was the Pretender ? The Pretender was a man who pretended he was heir to the English Crown, but was found out. He tried many times to get an army and to drive the English back, and then put himself on the Crown, but he was beaten every time. He landed in Ireland once, were he found such bad troops that he was frightened to meet the English, but he made an army and was beaten by the English.

Henry met Becket on the altar steps and severely massacred him.

Lady Jane Grey said she was content with her books, so she was beheaded.

Who was Harley ? Harley was a person on the side of the elector of Hanover. He was stabbed by a French adventurer whose name was the Baron de Guiscard in the ribs and thus got into favour he was much put down by the Duke of Marlborough.

Who were the Spartans ? The Spartans were very cruel. They used to hate the sight of a Helot. If they could catch one they would eat him raw, so it shews what a spite they had against them. They used to be governed by an oligarchy.

If the Premier dies, who officiates ? An undertaker.

Cranmer was burned for refusing to acknowledge Anne Boleyn as his wife.

Nelson's wife was, of course, Lady Nelson, but it was Lady Hamilton who made a husband of him.

When roused the British Lion is a very hard nut to crack.

The strength of the British Constitution lies in the fact that the Lords and the Commons cheek each other.

The guilds were the ancestors of trade unions, but now only old women go there to sew.

Henry VII passed a law saying that no man must have a liver.

Where are the descendants of the ancient Britons to be found to-day.   In the British Museum.

The Turks manicured the pilgrims.

The Gauls couldn't take the catapault because Manilus was awoke by the quacking of the holy ducks.

The Reform Bill was presented to Parliament.   It managed to pass three houses, but was then thrown out of the window.

The King of France was subject to no earthly control and no divine control that was perceptible.

Mary Queen of Scots was so beautiful that she didn't go south until her position was hopeless.

John Maynard (who was burnt to death), died from the effects of the fire upon his constitution.

Elizabeth is said to have stayed at a certain place at the back of St Andrew's church, and is still there.

Queen Victoria was one of the best reigners. When she died soldiers fighting in the Boer war left the war to come and see the last of her.

King Edward VII was the best king we ever had, because he hadn't the privilege of doing what he liked, and it was all the better for him.

Louis XVI was gelatined.

Describing the great fire.   The worst flaming place of all was St Paul's Cathedral.

Queen Elizabeth was a virgin queen, and she was never marrid. She was so fond of dresses that she was never seen without one on. She was beautefull and clever with a red hed and freckles.

William Pitt considered that he was a very suitable undertaker for the war with France.

Five Mile Act.   Every parson must preach more than five miles off his church.

Who was Henry VIII ? A great widower.

Universal suffrage means that even the illegible have votes.

The Pilgrim Fathers thought it better to be out of this wicked world and so colonised in Massachussets.

Rome is noted for its Catacombs, where skulls of great people are kept. These are very long and dismal.

The Fire of London, although looked on first as a calamity, really did a great deal of good. It purified the city from the dregs of the plague and burnt down eighty-nine churches.

King James the First was very unclean in his habits. He never washed his hands and married Anne of Denmark.

Henry VIII was a very good king. He liked plenty of money. He had plenty of wives and died of ulcers in the legs.

The Trial of the Seven Bishops. The bishops signed a partition and sent it to the king, and the king got very angry and would not sign the partition and ordered them to be hung, and they were all killed except one and he whent for the kings side.

The Seven Years' War. It went on and off in a funy sort of way until the seven years were up.

Describe briefly the character of James II : what children had he ? James was a bad tempered man and he had no children.

He went to public houses and got very drunk. He was rather a bad king ; he had rather a big tongue, some people say, and perhaps it is true. Mary, Charles I, and Charles II were the sons and daughters of James II.

James II was a very bad king, he had no children, and he ruled badly, and altogether he was a very bad king indeed.

Sir Phillip Sydney gave the last drop of water in his jog to a dying soldier on the field of Waterloo, as was mentioned in the Duke of Wellington's dispatches.

Clive was a soldier who did most of his public work in India and one day he went and took Arcot and Clive was beaten and a lot of his soldiers were stuffed in a black whole of Calcoter and most of them were suffercated, and a great cruelty it was thought.

A papal Bull gave you the alternative of obedience or of being excommunicated from the privileges of the Church. It is a Bull, with reference to the horns of a Dilemma. So an Irish Bull is a choice—you may believe it, or you may not believe it.

A Crusade was an early name for honeymoon.

The barons had family crests which everyone tried to live up to, but they were generally over the mantel-piece.

The Five Mile Act was passed by Queen Victoria to prevent loafing and drunkenness in public houses. People must prove that they had travelled five miles before they would be supplied with beer and spirits. That made people ashamed to get so drunk as before.

What was the South Sea Bubble? It was a manefacture which got awfully big but went down again. Some people had to pay a lot to get in.

The South Sea Bubble was a scream for lending money to the Government.

When Henry VIII took the throne, the older Catherine got, the less he liked her, because he said she was getting uglier, so he asked the Pope weather he ought to marry his brother's wife, thinking he'd say "no," but the Pope said it did not matter, for he had had her all these years, and that surprised him.

Lack of indiscretion was King Stephen's greatest personal enemy.

Finally James the Second gave birth to a son so the people turned him off the throne.

William gave the land to under vessels.

The "Root and Branch" Bill ordered farmers to prune their trees every year.

There is no doubt that Queen Elizabeth launched the basis of the British Navy and kept all her men at sea.

Westminster is remarkable for the number of laws that get past.

The King wore a scarlet robe trimmed with vermin.

Wolsey saved his life by dying on the way from York to London.

Henry VIII was very cruel to Ann Boleyn and ironed her.　　(Text book reading : " He pressed his suit on her.")

The chief duties of an M.P. are to go to sleep when another man is speaking, and force his party into power.

What might have happened if Edward the Confessor had not received the Crown ?　　He might have got half a crown.

After the great feasts, William I used to entertain the barons by letting off fireworks.

If William of Orange had not been defeated at the battle of Hastings the history of England would have taken a very different course.

Boadicæa walked through the town without any clothes on.
Boadicæa was Cæsar's wife.

William the Third before he became king was called Prince Orange of Rufus.

An Isolationist is a man who prefers making money by himself.

The Feudal System required that all liver's should be registered.

Boadicæa was a brave woman who fought herself and drove a chariot.

Philip had made England Roman Catholic, but when Elizabeth came to the throne England was made Christian.

The Chiltern Hundreds are the things you see with a microscope in cheese.

General Smuts are what all the different black races are called in the north-western quarter of Africa.

Oliver Cromwell was a brave strong leader but the greatest thing about him was the wart on his nose.

What is a Pretender ?   Write a few lines about the different Pretenders who have appeared in British history.   A " pretender " is someone who thinks he can do two things at once, but he can't.   Alfred the Great was a Pretender, because he pretended to look after the cakes and think of his enemies at the same time.

E

The Duke of Monmouth was found lying in a ditch, with some peas in his pocket which he had eaten.

The Pope called Henry " Fido, the Offensive." The Pope never did like Henry's wives, but then it wasn't his business to, being a Pope.

Charles II also wanted Parliament to maintain all his subjects in the freedom of their persons.

Essay on the Battle of Jutland. In my opinion Jellicoe's tactics were right and Beatty's wrong. I have no reason for saying this.

If you want to remember the names of the British leaders in the battle of Jutland, think of " J " for German and " B " for Bosh.

The Duke of Marlborough was a great general who always commenced a battle with the fixed determination to win or lose.

At Marston Moor you will never see a white rose. This shows what a lot of blood must have been shed before the English beat the Spaniards. They were really at the bottom of the League of Nations.

Clive committed suicide three times and the third time they sent him to India.

Drake knew all about the Armada before he saw it, so he was able to go on bowelling for some time.

Queen Elizabeth had two children Anne Boleyn and Henry the Eighth. When the King of Spain asked her to marry him she said, " No, Sire, I prefer to remain a virgin queen."

Henry said " Beware of the Brides of March."

The low wages paid by the farmers led to the pheasants' revolt.

The imflammability of the Pope was proclaimed in the Vatican decrees.

Clive imprisoned 146 men in the Black Hole of Calcutta and so laid the foundations of our Indian Empire.

We are still confronted with a choice between Free Trade and Detection.

" Habeas Corpus " was a phrase of the Great Plague and means " Bring out your dead."

Perkin Warbeck was saying he was the son of a king, but really he was the son of respectable parents.

During the Napoleonic Wars crowned heads were trembling in their shoes.

Cardinal Wolsey died at Leicester, saying : If I had served my king as he served me, he would never have lived to an old age.

St Andrews is the patent saint of Scotland.   The patent saint of England is Union Jack.

The first Roman sent to Britain was very cross with the people for not being Christians.

The synod of Whitby was about what shape the tonsil on the priest's head should be cut.

Politicians turn to and fro in their perplexity, weaving and unweaving their combinations.

The Ballot Act said that all voting must be done by voting.

In Elizabeth's reign Parliament frequently interfered and urged the sovereign to marry, a thing it would not have dreamt of doing in the reign of Henry VIII.

Queen Philippa saved the lives of six honest burglars of Calais.

William the Conqueror was one of our best authors and wrote the Doomsday Book.

Lambert Simnel became a scorpion in Henry's kitchen.

Oliver Cromwell was captain of an ironclad.

Queen Elizabeth's face was thin and pale, but she was a stout Protestant.

Purchase Tax was imposed to make people realise they were paying for something they weren't getting.

Rehabilitation means dressing a soldier in clothes he wouldn't have otherwise.

Edward I had a son born at Carnarvon Castle, namely Edward II, the remains are still to be seen.

Women's suffrage is the state of suffering to which they are born.

Magna Carta said that the King had no right to bring soldiers into a lady's house and tell her to mind them.

The Rump Parliament consisted of Cromwell's stalactites.

When England was placed under an Interdict the Pope stopped all births, deaths, and marriages for a year.

The leading cause of the English Reformation was that the Pope insisted upon Henry VIII employing massage for the dead.

The Gunpowder plot was an awful thing. It was done to kill the King and Parliament. It is still done on the 5th of November.

Margaret of Anjou was fat since she was one of Henry's stoutest supporters.

The ancient Britons used to fish in cockles (? coracles) and used to paint their faces so that they would know one another if they were drowned.

In 1947 everybody's lights were cut, but politicians soon got so tired of candles that their gas was soon restored.

William the Conqueror landed in 1066 A.D. and A.D. means after dark.

In olden times foresters used to wear halibuts under their necks.

England wanted to keep Flanders and Gascony as it traded in wool and wine respectfully with these parts.

The Black Prince's health was waisted through lack of proper food and clothes.

George Prince of Wales was incognito but of course every one knew that familiar figure under the pose of "Duk of Summersett."

Henry III's chief complaint was inviting foreigners to England.

Maria Theresa was a very clever empress. She prophesied about the future and put her prophesy in a box and said the box was to be opened in the presence of seven bishops.

Julius Cæsar was King of Rome, and a soothsayer told him to " beware the eyes of March."

Henry V asked Catherine for a kiss, but she said " In France, it is not right for a gentleman to kiss a lady before they are married." But in England it is just the other way round, so he did.

The Crusaders went all over England and made it fertile.

A National Government is one in which all parties forget themselves.

Lord Bacon was impeached for receiving brides.

A Tory is a politician who is definitely one-sided.

Basic petrol means what you can get away with without being stopped.

MEDICAL AND ANIMAL

A ruminating animal is one that chews its cubs.

The principal parts of the eye are the pupil, the moat, and the beam.

Food is nourished in the stomach. It is digested by the lungs. Digestion is brought on by the lungs having something the matter with them. The food then passes from your windpipe to your pores, and passes off your body by evaporation.

Germs are sort of small insecks that swim in you when they can get in. Some are called measles but you can't see them.

Anæmia is not having blood enough, but you have enough to bleed as much as anyone else if you cut your finger.

The office of the gastric juice is in the stomach.

Moths eat least of all because they eat holes.

A halibut is a combined spear and battle axe.

A lynx is an animal of the cat family; its skin is spotted with very sharp eyes.

How do you spell "hair" when you mean "rabit"?

A hostage is a big bird with four legs and a long neck.

A cat is a quadruped, the legs, as usual, being at the four corners.

To keep milk from turning sour you should keep it in the cow.

To kill a butterfly you pinch its borax.

By eating food slowly it is digested before it is swallowed, and thus it enriches the blood which goes down one leg and up the other.

The tiger is a very veracious animal.

An elephant is a square animal with a tail in front and behind.

Doctors now treat patients with ultra-violent rays.

A mosquito is the child of black and white parents.

A cosmetic is for making people sick.

A cuckoo is a bird what lays other birds eggs in its own nest, and *viva voce*.

The chief disease affecting the veins is plebiscite.

Psychology is a modern disease, generally seen in twitching.

There are two oracles in the heart—the right oracle and the left oracle.

There are three spaces in the body; the head, chest and trunk, holding respectfully the brain, heart and vowels.

What is a coroner? A man whose duty is to decide whether a person died a natural or a fatal death.
He crowns the King.
He is likely one of the King's men who plays on the coronet at banquets, or accompanies the yeomanry.
They are persons who look after crowns.
He is an under-general and he must obey his higher subjects.

Blood consists of two kinds of corkscrews — red corkscrews and white corkscrews.

Panel doctors are different from ordinary doctors, they are paid.
Panel doctors are supposed to charge their patients nothing for what they give them.

An oculist is a fish with long pegs.

Guano is the product of manurous birds.

The zebra is a sort of cream-coloured donkey with black stripes from which they make grate-polish.

The zebra is like the horse only striped, and is chiefly used to illustrate the letter Z.

The cammel is the ship of the dessert.

The cow is the foundation of milk and coffee.

Ladies chase the mackeral in their fishing smacks until they get them into Yarmouth Harbour, and there they catch them and bring in stacks of these fish.

If the steelyard had not been invented the cow would have had to be cut up before it could be weighed.

Our food was eaten and our water was drunken.

Who were the Dispensers ?   People who tested liquids (milk, etc.).

Palsy is a kind of new writer's dance.

The only pouched animal in America is the apostle.

The cow has a pulse as well as anyone else, but you can't feel it in its wrist.

Blood flows through the alimentary canal into the abdominal canopy.

Herrings go about the sea in shawls.

When a person is susceptible to something they are called septic.   Girls in love often are.

The sweetbread is called the Pancreas, being named after the Midland Railway station which is in London.

We should not eat too much bone-making food, because if we do we shall have too many bones, and that would make us look funny.

The larynx is a voice box and shuts when we swallow it.

There are many eligible fish in the North Sea.

The dodo is a bird that is nearly decent now.

Rabies is what you put round a dog's nose to prevent his biting.

The liver is an infernal organ.

Lovers call the heart the seat of love, but doctors take a more detached view.

The best food for babies is oxygen, hydrogen and a little carbon.

The symptoms of scarlet fever are a very bad sore throat and interruptions on the face.

Soups for invalids may be made by bones, and pieces of meet, and gently simmered for a long time, then the meat is strained off and called soup. But the pieces of meat should be allowed to run out when they can't be kept in.

There are four symptoms of a cold, two I forget and the other two are well-known. I would treat a cold in this manner, by rubbing a rough towel, or a coarse flesh brush.

The heart is a big working machine. It pumps up the impure blood and the pure blood down the other side. It is full of bright red blood and all over the rest of the bodies we have only dirty blood. You can easily tell a drunkard's heart it is fat all over, but a good heart is all nice and lean.

The best thing for a drowned person is to tie their tongue under their chin and make them walk about, or else keep them warm, and give them something better than brandy.

A drug is any wholesome vegetable good for taking once in a way, but not for regular food.

An injection is a shout or scream raised by a person too surprised or frightened to make a sentence with his thoughts. It is not quite a human language. The lower animals say nothing else but injections. Accordingly ill-natured and cross people by their injections come very near to beasts.

A skeleton is a man with his inside out and his outside off.

It is pain to a cat to tread on its paw, and it swears, but in a different manner to what we do.

When you stroke a cat by drawing your hand along its back it cocks its tail up like a ruler, so as you can't get no further.

Cats have nine lives, but which is seldom required in this country coz of Christianity.

Father has been in bed with an allegory in his leg.

Artificial respiration is what you make a person alive with when they are only just dead.

Phlebitis is a disease frequently taken by people looking after menageries.

Respiration is composed of two acts, first inspiration and then expectoration.

Why does a horse wear blinkers ?   So that he shan't see father.

What is a microbe ?   A robe that the mics wear.

Letter to master : " Please sir, I can't get to school as mother is in bed with ten disciples." (Appendicitis.)

Please sir, Billy's ill with swellings in his throat, and the doctor says it's gathering of the clans.

Some people frequently lose their consciences when they are very ill.

What are rabies, and what would you do for them ? Rabies are Jewish priests. I should do nothing for them.

The bloodvessels are the veins, arteries and artilleries.

The stomach is the most delated part of the elementary canal.

Lumbago is a mineral used for making pencils.

The heart is over the ribs in the middle of the thorax.

Man is the only animal who can strike a light.

Tadpoles eat one another and become frogs.

The different kinds of senses are commonsense and nonsense.

Some cows are very dangerous, especially the bull.

The animal which possess the greatest attachment for man is woman.

Quinine is the bark of a tree : canine is the bark of a dog.

A bloodvessel is a man's lifeboat.

A sheep is mutton covered with wool.

The home of the swallow is the stomach.

He has gone to Switzerland to remunerate his health.

A cat is a carnation because he eats meat.

The heart is a comical bag divided into four parts by a fleshy petition.

A sure-footed animal is an animal that when it kicks it does not miss.

The liver is situated south of the stomach.

Marsupials are poached animals.

Sonambulist : A man who writes a novel.   A very clever person.

The doctor who visits our office has assigned to me the month of March for my recovery.

Pasteurized milk comes from Pasteur. He was French, but now his milk has gone so far that he is really international.

Magnesium is the best food for babies. It will stop almost anything.

MUSIC

The fugue is what you get in a room full of people when all the windows and doors are shut.

An oboe is an American tramp.

An octet is a figure with eight sides.

Scales are of two kinds—diatonic and rheumatic.

There are two kinds of scales, dramatic and chronic.

A chromatic scale is formed entirely of semi-circles.

Syncopation is emphasis on a note that is not in the piece.

Melba—where Napoleon was imprisoned.

Some instruments used in the orchestra are: viles, cellars, trumpets, hornets, baboons, old boys and bubble bases.

Mandolines are high officials in China.

Handel wrote fairy tails.

Euclid wrote lovely music.

A sonatina is an instrument which you play by pulling it in and out.

The gamut is a musical scale. The name is derived from gamut or catgut, the material from which the strings of instruments used to be made.

One semibrieve equals two minions and one crochet four semi-skews.

A man who looks on the bright side of things is called an optimist, and one who looks on the dull side is called a pianist.

D.C.   Don't clap !

F.R.C.O.   Fellow of Royal Canine Office.

Two crotchets make a quaker.

There are two pedals, the soft and the hard.

Interpretation is the way you present a piece of piece to other people.

To descant is to pour out the air above the tune.

Three-four time is simply cripple time.

A trio must be sung three times up to the word D.C.

A dot lengthens a note one semitone.

Esipodical form is when one tune goes out while the other comes in.

Contralto is a low sort of music that only ladies sing.

Silence in music is shown by putting your feet down on the paddles.

My favourite instrument is the picadilly.

Beethoven is found in *The Radio Times*. He made 38 senators and lately celebrated his centurion death. His father was a drunkard and sang Bass.

Crooning is a modern form of singing derived from sub-animal or vegetable sources.

An instrumentalist is one who plays his instrument for love.

Handel wrote the " Messiah " and later " The Lost Chord." It is the latter people cannot forget.

SCIENCE AND MATHEMATICS

A thermometer is for measuring how much water there is in milk, a hydrometer for measuring how much milk there is in water.

A thermometer is an instrument for raising temperance.

Gravity was discovered by Isaac Walton. It is chiefly noticeable in the autumn, when the apples are falling off the trees.

Gravity is that which if there were none we should all fly away.

The Law of Gravetation demands that the grass in every town churchyard shall be cut once every year.

Newton brought us the theory of gravitation, and now we cannot do without our large gravitation supply.

Gravitation is a limit of ten miles an hour.

Gravity tells us why an apple does not go to heaven.

A parallel straight line is one that when produced to meet itself does not meet.

Parallel lines are those which when they are produced so as they meet, do not meet.

Parallel lines are lines which if produced to eternity will then meet.

The process of turning steam into water again is called Conversation.

Question : Define a circle.   Answer : Take your centre and take your distance and draw a straight curved line. This is a circle and all lines drawn to it are equal.

A circle is a line of no depth running round a dot for ever.

A circle is a round straight line with a hole in the middle.

A circle is a round line with no kinks in it, joined up so as not to show where it began.

An obtuse-angled triangle is a solid three-sided figure with thick sides.

To remove air from a flask, fill the flask with water, tip the water out, and put the cork in quick.

A vacuum is an empty space where the Pope lives.

A vacuum is a U-tube with a flask at one end.

Acid is a compound which will redden venerable blues.

A barometer is a place built on the roof of a house where men go to study the stars.

The Zodiac is the Zoo of the sky where lions, goats, virgins and other animals go after they are dead.

To germinate is to become a naturalised German.

A litre is a nest of young puppies.

Chlorine gas is very injurious to the human body, and the following experiments should, therefore, only be performed on the teacher.

A centimetre is an insect with a hundred legs.

Polygon—a man with several wives.

A pollygon is a dead parrot.

Protractors cannot be used for taking up potatoes.

Hydrogen is colourless, odourless and insolvent.

Atomic weights are used for weighing atoms.

Infinity is a place where no one can get to but all lines meet.

A vacuum is nothing shut up in a box. They have a way of pumping out the air. When all the air and everything else is shut out, naturally they are able to shut in nothing, where the air was before.

Two straight lines cannot enclose a space unless they are crooked.

A quotation is the answer to a division sum.

A surface is the very top you cannot see.

Ice—Water that went to sleep in the cold.

Liquids expand when heated—e.g. if a kettle is placed on the fire with water in it and all means of ventilation stopped up, the kettle would bounce off the fire from the great force which was made inside in which it wanted to let escape.

Algebra was the wife of Euclid.

Average means something that hens lay eggs on.

Pythagoras was known as the personification of the transmission of souls and the inventor of the right-angled triangle.

The line opposite the right angle in a right-angled triangle is called the hippopotamus.

A line in geometry is what you draw and do not see.

A line is a length of breath.

Define a point. A point is that which has no magnitude, but only length and breadth : and there is a point in a circle where all straight lines are equal.

Water is composed of two gins, Oxygin and Hydrogin. Oxygin is pure gin, Hydrogin is gin and water.

The end of parabola will never meet, though, of course, this could be done by making one small enough.

Things which are halves of themselves are equal to each other.

Algebraical symbols are those used when you do not know what you are talking about.

Water may be made hard by freezing, and the hardness removed by boiling it.

A rectangle is much larger than an acute angle.

Philosophy increases thirty-two feet per second.

Explanation of *reductio ad absurdum* : " The proof of the proposition is begun by supposing some- thing which is impossible . . . the proof ends up wrongly."

There are 90 right-angles in 180 degrees.

Heat is transmitted by conviction.

A horse-power is measured by the distance a horse can carry a pound of water in an hour.

A trapezium is the thing in the gymnasium.

Sodium nitrate is the chief chilly sauce of nitric acid.

A triangle with equal sides is called equatorial.

What is a ratio ?   Half the diameter of a circle.

When a graph of y equals x^2 is plotted, what is the resultant curve ?   An eclipse.

The weight of one square centimeter is put upon it.

Geometry teaches us to bisex angels.

Isosceles triangles are used on maps to join up places with the same weather.

A prism is a kind of dried plum, because people say "prunes and prisms."

A Theorem—derived from "theos," a god, a "res," a thing—is a problem needing Divine intelligence.

A solid is that which has no space under the circumference.

Explain the word "asset."   When you are making out an account you subtract the smaller from the larger amount.   That is called assetaining the difference.

The difference between air and water is that air can be made wetter, but water cannot.

Things which are equal to each other are equal to anything else.

Vanishing lines are those that get nearer together as they get further apart.

A magnetic force is a straight line, generally a curved one, which would tend to point to where the North Pole comes.

The " Complete Angler " is another name for Euclid because he wrote all about angles.

A magnet is a thing you find in a bad apple.

Ammonium chloride is also called silly maniac.

Parallel lines are the same distance all the way and cannot meet unless you bend them.

A parallelepiped is an animal with parallel legs.

The mechanical advantage of a long pump handle is that you can have someone to help you pump.

An observatory is a factory where clocks are made.

We are now masters of steam and eccentricity.

How would you make soft water hard ?   Freeze it.

If the sum of two angles is equal to two right angles, what name is given to the angles ?   Complimentary.
If the sum of the angles is one right angle, what are they called ?   Uncomplimentary.

To find the centre of gravity of a sheet of cardboard, suspend a Plimsoll line from a pin.

At $180C$. sulphur is vicious.

Allotropes are the parts that a substance can be split up into and are much smaller than an atom.

A curve is the longest way between two points.

To find the area of the walls of a room you take the barometer and multiply by the height.

CO_2 is used for keeping people from dyeing and for distinguishing fires.

A compass tells a man where he ought to go and always points to the sun.

Oxygen is collected by a new Matric. trough.
Oxygen can be prepared by heating potassium chocolate.
An oxygen has eight sides.
Oxygen is the stuff of which oxo is made.

Air is made up of oxygen and sanatogen.

To find the squares on the side of a triangle you have to square the hypothesis.

An issocciles triangle is one with three of its sides equal but not parallel.

Water freezes at a higher temperature on the Fahrenheit thermometer than on a Centigrade.

Ether is everywhere except between programs, so then London takes a little piano music until it comes back.

Induction is what they do to curates.

What is the half of five ? It depends whether you mean the two or the three.

Nitric acid burns yellow holes in your clothes.

We degenerate CO_2 by the action of sulphuric acid on marble.

Ignition is the art of noticing.

If the air contains more than 100% carbolic acid it is very injurious to health.

Inertia is that which tends to have a uniform motion in a state of rest.

Resistance is of two kinds, passive and leased. Leased resistance is a line to a thing the easiest way.

Our school is ventilated by hot currants.

Mass is the amount of matter in a human body.

The Davy safety lamp depends on the safety of the miners, because of the dangerous gas, for it kills the men who are working down the shaft.

The principal of the aneroid barometer is that it has a corrugated vacuum.

In 400 B.C. a man said nature does not abhor a vacuum.

Radiation is standing in front of a fire without the interviewing median being heated.

To fill an apparatus with acidulated water, turn on the taps and acidulate.

Explain the meaning of "erg."   When people are playing football and you want them to do their best you erg them on.

Science is material; religion is immaterial.

When you look in a mirror the angel of incidence equals the angel of reflection.

It is easy to stall a car if you open your throttle before you are engaged.

LITERATURE AND GRAMMAR

The diminutive of man is mankind.

Define the first man.   Answer : Adam.

Explain the word "fetish."   It is applied to persons who seem to have a gay air, as if they were going to a fête.

Explain "mortgage."   When people do not wish their diseased relatives to be buried, they send them to a mortuary to have their remains mortgaged.

A monologue is a dialogue for one person.

Robert Burns, in 1787 became literally a lion.

Paraphrase "O God of Battles, steel my soldiers' hearts, possess them not with fear."   "O Mars, rob my soldiers of their hearts and don't be afraid to keep them."

John Wyclif was the editor of the *Morning Star*, but afterwards became a reformer.

The feminine of manager is managerie.

The wife of a duke is a ducky.

Impervious means saturated without overflowing, like a drunkard or a sponge before they are squeezed.

Explain the word " buttress."   A woman who makes butter.   A female butcher.

Teacher's dictation : " His choler rose to such a height that passion well nigh choked him."   Pupil's reproduction : " His collar rose to such a height that fashion well nigh choked him."

" The Golden Horn " and " The Golden Fleece " are the names of public houses.

The masculine of Duchess is duck.

The feminine of drake ?   Queen Elizabeth.

Bacon was the man who thought he wrote Shakespeare.

A period is a dot at the end of a sentence.   Period costumes are dresses all covered with dots.

Tennyson, the greatest prose writer that ever lived, wrote the " Iliad," and " Paradise Lost."

" Dour " means a sort of help, as in the hymn " O God dour help in ages past."

A metaphor is a strong way of saying polite things, such as would be called swearing by uneducated people.

An Irish bull is a male cow.

" Essays of Elia." The attempts of Elijah to get food.

A relative pronoun is a family pronoun, such as " mother," " brother," " aunt."

Joan of Arc was cannonised by Bernard Shaw.

Theseus begged Minos to try and kill the labrynth.

Sir Walter Scott wrote " Quentin Durwood," " Ivanhoe," and " Emulsion."

Examinations may be written or *vice versa*.

In his journey up Mount Zion Christian had a fight with a polygon.

Mephistopheles was a Greek comic poet.

What is Milton's chief work ? Milton wrote a sensible poem called " The Canterbury Tales."

Give the names of five of Shakespear's plays. " Macbeth," " Mikado," " Quo Vadie," " San Toy," " The Sign of the Cross."

A Cæsura (in verse) is when a foot has more than two halves.

The Augustan era was a mistake of Augustus.

Walter Scott was imprisoned in the Tower because he could not pay his debts. While there he wrote the Waverley Novels, but he was afterwards burnt alive. He also brought tobacco from Virginia, so called after his beloved mistress Queen Elizabeth.

Describing Tom Sawyer (Mark Twain). He was a smart looking boy, very fond of fighting, and he was always sharp at this kind of job. His character was always good sometimes.

Of Charles Lamb. It was his sister and him who essayed most of Shakespeare's writings. Another : It was Mary Lamb with Charles who between them wrote most of Shakespeare's fairy tales.

Oliver Twist had a very good effect, for people saw the workhouses in a different limelight.

Degrees of comparison of " Bad." Bad : very sick : dead.

The masculine of dam is dash.

John Ridd was very kind to his sisters and all other dumb animals.

Shakespeare married Anne Hathaway, who it seems, lived up to her name, and had her own way and gave Shakespeare a hot time of it.

Cæsar's wife was above —— ? Forty.

G

Saturnine means gloomy-looking, sad.   Saturn was the god of agriculture.

The brave knight was swallowed up by the awful abbess that yawned all of a sudden in front of him.

Quadrupeds has no singular, you cannot have a horse with one leg.

Wordsworth wrote The Imitations of Immorality.

Chesterton committed suicide at Bristol.   He was only nineteen and very thin and hungry.

The Possessive Case is the case when somebody has got yours and won't give it up.

The plural of penny is twopence.

In the sentence " I saw the goat butt the man," " butt " is a conjunction because it shows the connection between the goat and the man.

Masculine, man ; feminine, woman ; neuter, corpse.

Milton wrote " Paradise Lost," then his wife died and he wrote " paradise regained."

The altar was decked with harem lilies which have always been an emblem of purity.

Pope wrote principally in heroic cutlets.

What meter is Tennyson's "Ulysses" written in? In diameter. Thermometer. It is written in meterphor.

Milton when he was twelve years old wrote a hymn beginning, "Letters from a Gladstone mind."

Describe the figure of speech or artifice of style used in the following: "The child is father to the man." Answer: "This was written by Shakespeare. He often made this kind of mistake."

Correct the following: a. A hen has three legs. b. Who done it? One small boy, evidently thinking there was some hidden connection between the two, answered: "The hen never done it, God done it."

Most of Shakespeare's plays were terrible tragedies.

Coleridge was a retired mariner who took to verse.

Wordsworth's poetry is too full of thoughts to be natural. His descriptions of sunsets are natural, but rural.

Samuel Johnson was known as the Doctor of Difinity because he wrote the first dictionary.

"The lark that soars on dewy wing" means that the lark was going so high and flapping his wings so hard that he broke into perspiration.

> "Beneath whose awful hand we hold
> Dominion over rod and line."

Essay extract : On Sunday father misjudged a woman crossing the road.

Homer wrote the Oddity.

Shakespeare wrote the Merry Widow.

The Gorgons were three sisters that lived in the islands of the Hesperides somewhere in the Indian Ocean. They had long snakes for hair, tusks for teeth, and claws for nails, and they looked like women only more horrible.

Feminines : Bear, vixen ; Sheep, you.   Masculine of ladybird : The masculine of ladybird sounds as if it ought to be gentlemanbird, but that looks funny.

An abstract noun is something you can't see when you are looking at it.

Vergel was a man who used to clean up churches.

Virgil was in love with a girl named Enid and wrote a lot of books about her.

The masculine of vixen is vicar.

Poetry is a thing you make prose of.

The masculine of heroine is kipper.

A conjunction is a place where two railway lines meet.

An anachronism is a thing a man puts in writing in the past before it has taken place in the future.

Some writers put too many conjunctions in their work, which becomes a disease known as conjunctivitis.

What is the last letter of the English alphabet? Yours truly. (From a Japanese pupil.)

Shakespeare ran away to London and worked outside a picture palace.

St George saved a little girl from a monstrous dragoon.

An iambic pentameter is a five sided figure with equal sides.

A demagogue is a vessel from which one drinks beer.

" What angle wakes me from my floury bed ? "

I have an idea that Goldsmith, the poet, was rather a jockular fellow.

Did any of the poems you read make you feel angry or miserable?   The poem of the Forsaken Merman made me very angry, to think that a woman could leave a poor helpless man to get his own meals.

Byron wrote epics and swam the Hellespont.   In between he made love drastically.

King Arthur was a person who was washed up when a baby, and Merlin said it should be so, and they proved it.

" A little learning is a dangerous thing
Drink deep, or taste not the aperient spring."

Literary criticism.
" She hase virgins many
Fresh and Fair
Yet you are more sweat than any."
I like this poem because it describes the violets ever so well.

From an essay. I stood on the cliff, the sea was ruff and the wind roared and not a sole was to be seen.

When Achilles heard the sad news, he pulled all his hair out and put on dust instead.

Bassanio sang a beautiful song called, " Tell me, where is fancy bread ? "

What is, in your opinion, the actual value of analysis ? To know where to put the verb and subject etc, in analysis is something for a boy to be proud of.

When you start to do a piece of analysis you say to yourself where am I going to put the sentences and then you put them there which is a very good exercise.

Fluellen is particular to wear a leak on St David's Day.

In the quarrel between Oberon and Titania I cannot waste any sympathy over Oberon because he should have known better than start to argue with a woman.

Lady Macbeth, hearing the clock strike, exclaimed, " Out, damned spot ! "

Hood was a poet who always sang songs in his shirt. He was no madder than most poets.

Scheherazade was Bluebeard's wife for a thousand nights, so no wonder she was able to tell her famous tales.

Who were the Lotus Eaters ?   They were ship-wrecked mariners and the natives kept them on a patent mixture that had been passed down.   It was so good that they ate it and kept on at it.

Which of Dr Johnson's characteristics are you disposed to criticise ?   I criticise him for his corpulency for it was not natural fatness and he could have helped it.

Explain, "He fell a victim to the fascinations of the siren."   A siren is a disease.

Socrates used to walk about on the ice without boots and it made ever so many of the people ashamed of him.

No one yet has succeeded in edifying the dark lady of the sonnets.

Plato was the god of the Underground.

Cassandra was a Trojan profiteer.

Baccus first taught the Greeks to get drunk and Raleigh named tobacco after him in honour of the Virgin Queen.

Well's history is a veritable mill stone on the road to learning.

An autobiography is the life of an animal written after it is dead as a moral.

An abstract noun is one that cannot be heard, seen, touched, or smelt.

An interjection is a sudden explosion of mind.

The plural of spouse is spice.

A metaphor is a suppressed smile.

Tennyson wrote a most beautiful poem called, "In Memorandum."

Explain an epigram.   Something spoken at the end of a play.   Something put on the outside of an envelope. A conundrum.

A consonant is a large piece of land surrounded by water.

An epitaph is a short sarcastic poem.

Written of the literature of the 18th century. Much of the poetry of this period was superfluous, and written in artificial language.

The bowels are a, e, i, o, u, and sometimes w and y.

Milton's poems are pleasant to read, but being strict Puritan, throughout the whole of his poems there is nothing to promote laughter.

A sentence that does not depend on any word in the sentence is not subordinate but inordinate.

Shakespeare wrote tragedies, comedies and errors.

Chaucer wrote the Arabian Knights who were holy men like Prince Arthur etc, that made pilgrimages to Canterbury and told tales round a table.

A child's explanation of " rhetorical question." It is when a lot of questions are asked and there is no answer to it. Example : " What has the Prime Minister been doing all these years ? "

Do you think Shylock was necessarily a bad character ? No because after all he had his living to make.

A simile is a picturesque way of saying what you really mean, such as calling your mother an old trout.

From an essay on Shakespeare. There are some passages in Shakespeare's work, which are quite pretty, as " Spoil the rod, and bare the child," and lots of others.

" Ster " is a female suffix, as will be seen in spinster, monster and sterile.

When a word gets out of date it is termed " dead " and so gradually a language is built up.

The plural of forget-me-not is forget-us-not.

In conclusion we may say that Shylock was greedy, malicious, and indeed, entirely viscous.

Give a sentence containing the word " summit." There is summit the matter.

A " case " means something that is going on in the police court. It was a bad case and the lawyer went to defend the case.

Spinster and lobster are the only nouns which preserve the feminine force of the suffix " ster."

The masculine of lass is ass.

Shakespeare lived at Windsor with his merry wives.

Diæresis is a mark under *a, o, u,* to give them the sound of *s.*

Polonius was a mythical sausage.

" I took thee for thy better."   This was said by Hamlet when he stabbed Polonius and thought it was a rat.

Omnipotence means having too many presents, like Father Christmas.

Transparent means something you can see through, for instance, a keyhole.

A phlegmatic person is one who has chronic broncitis.

From an essay.   We had a box of canimals.

When we got there our trunk hadn't arrived, so we had to sleep in something else.

Near the corpse a mansion rose.

An incomplete thought is called a frays.

After twice committing suicide Cowper lived till 1800 when he died a natural death.

What is a Blue Stocking ?   A stocking that is blue instead of black or brown.   One who is a knight of the Garter.

Who was Charon ?   Charon was the man who fried soles over the sticks.

The best book I have ever read was lamb's tails from Shakespear.

A collation is a kind of food, or the putting of a vicar into his new church. This is known as a cold collation.

Describing a scene in " Uncle Tom's Cabin." " Toby grinned at Miss Ophelia, displacing a beautiful set of white teeth."

What do you know of King Arthur ?   King Arthur collected all the fine brave good-looking young men of his time and called them The Knuts of the Round Table.

Dealing with Hiawatha the teacher explained that he left Olive with his grandmother as his father lived far away in the Rocky mountains.   Next day, a scholar retold the story thus : Hiawatha had Olive with his grandmother as his father could not keep him because he was on the rocks.

In an essay describing a picture.   By the side of the shepherd is an old sheep dog who had much over-lived.

Essay extract (from a boy who became an Eton Scholar) : Never shall I forget seeing a boy make 181 not out against a supposedly invisible side.

During reading a small boy, instead of saying "The bubble burst," said "The bubble bust." The teacher told him that he must never say "Bust," always "burst." Some days later the boy read aloud, "The burst of George Washington."

Lord Macauley suffered from gout and wrote all his poems in iambic feet.

Rhetoric is a form of arithmetic.

An epigram is a man who goes from one country to another.

A proposition is for a country to have no alcolic drinks in it.

Poetry is when every line starts with a capital letter.

The stoics were the disciples of Zero and believed in nothing much.

I have searched for the missing book in every room, and in each case the search was fatal.

"Onomatopœia" is a figure of speech making an invention long before its time, e.g. the clock struck one.

"Would he were fatter." These words were spoken by Brutus's wife when he was going about half-naked and worried and hardly ate any food.

Portia, the wife of Brutus, killed or poisoned herself by swallowing burning sticks.

Cassius was a vile selfish man who was always doing his best to make his own ends meet.

I can't remember his name, but it was a poet who talked of the first fine careless rupture.

Casabianca is a Moroccan watering place, but actually the rainfall isn't high.

From an essay.   There are many beautiful walks in the neighbourhood. . . . You first pass the Semetary and shortly after you come to the Imbersiles Home.

Write a sentence showing clearly the meaning of " posterity."
He had a cat, but nothing else lived on his posterity.
The man look as if he had been reduced to posterity.
Henry pade the fare because of his posterity.
By his clothes he seemed a person of great posterity.
The cat leaped about and then sat on its posterity.

Hood wrote things called skites on other people's poems.

There was a town which had hundreds of rates and mice and they could not get rid of them. One day a piper said he would get rid of the rates for a sum of money, so he played three notes on his pipe and the rates flocked out of the houses.

Kingsley was a baker and wrote on " Yeast."

Tolstoi was leader of the Passive Resisters. He had his goods sold rather than be vaccinated.

Socrates died from an overdose of wedlock.

The sere and yellow leaf is another name for tobacco.

Essay extract : A horn sounded and we were struck in the back. A lady was evidently trying to pass.

A metaphor is a thing you shout through.

George Eliot left a wife and children to mourn his genii.

The Press to-day is the mouth-organ of the people.

Gender is the destruction of sex.

The future of " I give " is " You take."

Tennyson wrote a poem called " Grave's Energy."

The Deserted Traveller is the most important of Goldsmith's works.

You cannot tell the gender of " egg " until it is hatched.

The appendix is a part of a book for which nobody ever found a use.

To excavate means to hollow out, e.g. " our baby excavates when he gets hurt."

Bunyan was the inventor of the Nonconformist religion, and also wrote Pilgrim's Chorus.

Ovid wrote a poem called the Medea which was lost fortunately.

The lady who witnessed my signature is not my mother and is therefore a credible witness.

The following is supposed to be in the style of Swift's " Gulliver's Travels." After some time we began falling with great velosity and then intrepidity, and we became so intrepidious that there was a crash.

From an essay on " A Walking Tour." I find some consolation in seeing an unused pump by the roadside. I swallow a few gulps of Nature's drink and lie down in a neighbouring corpse.

Keats was taken on the Mediterranean by the poet Sherry.

Shakespeare married Anne Hathaway, but he mostly lived at Windsor with his merry wives. This is quite usual with actors.

The old motality plays were the birth of the theatre but as boys took the girls' parts they were not nearly as moral as you might think.

PHILOSOPHY

A Job's comforter is a thing you give babies to sooth them.

An optimist is a man who looks after your eyes, a pessimist looks after your feet.

The millennium is the belief of the Freemasons.

An aristocrat is a man who performs tricks on the stage.

A pessimist is a man who is never happy unless he is miserable ; even then he is not pleased.

A philosopher is a man who makes the best of a bad job. Socrates is called a philosopher because he didn't worry much when he was poisoned.

A talisman is a man who calls every week for the furniture money.

Fallacy is another name for suicide.

The boy who looks at the future before it arrives can then look back at the past.

If life were all honey there would be nothing to live for.

What was Adam's punishment ?   He was to keep Eve.

But for a lucky stroke he (Fabre) might have been an insignificant schoolmaster.

Her mother, being immortal, had died.

Punctuality is hard to remedy once it is firmly established in the system.

Necessity is the mother of convention.

Epics describe the brave deeds of men called epicures.

Ambiguity means telling the truth when you don't mean to.

An emolument is a soothing medicine.

Liberty of conscience means doing wrong and not worrying about it afterwards.

Genius is an infinite capacity for picking brains.

Things which are impossible are equal to one another.

Chivalry is when you feel cold.

To-day many people are in jail for committing suicide while under the influence of drink.

The teetotaller is strong and has a better chance of getting on than the drinker, who is fat and flabby, and stands at the street corners all his life.

Seafaring men in the habit of drinking are liable to collide with other vessels.

The Salic Law is that you must take everything with a grain of salt.

Describe an abstract noun. It is the name of something which has no existence, as goodness.

Explain the phrase "missing the mark." This means a woman who hasn't got a man.

What is a mediator? A man who says, "Punch me instead."

What constitutes a Gentleman? (Standard VII composition). People sometimes think that when men are dressed in nice clothes they are gentlemen but that is not the case, a gentleman is a man who knows his manners. Down in the West End and City there are great swells, but people think that because they have nice clothes they are swells, but some are more like pigs. We might see a tramp walking along a street who has hardly no boots nor clothes but very likely he has his manners. A real gentleman ought to know his manners and also not to swear.

A sleeping partner is a man who goes to sleep playing bridge.

If you are drinking anything you should not pour it in your saucer but drink it by the handle.

H*

If a gentleman is out with his wife or sweetheart he should walk on the curve.

Widows should be cleaned sometimes.

Always choose a good neighbour, and if you are lucky enough to get a bath, have it at once.

If I pass in front of a person I have to say "Excise me!"

What is the difference between a window and a widow? You can see through a window——.

A passive verb is when the subject is the sufferer, as "I am loved."

If a man takes alcohol, his wife and children suffer, and *vice versa*.

Men are what women marry.

A surname is the name of a person you say "Sir" to.

When a man who is of sound mind commits suicide, the jury, instead of saying he did it in a fit of temporary insanity, bring in a verdict of *sine qua non*.

Everybody needs a holiday from one year's end to another.

A profiteer is a four-legged animal.

A pessimist is a man who professes to be a dentist.

Celibacy is the name of a great man.

Faith. That quality which enables us to believe what we know to be untrue.

A heretic is one who would never believe what he was told but only after seeing it and hearing it himself with his own eyes.

Income is a yearly tax.

A cynic is a man who refuses to believe fairy tales.

In the houses of the poor the drains are in a fearful state and quite unfit for human habitation.

A street is a road that has a very good class of people in it.

A connosieur is a man who stands outside the picture palace.

It takes three generations to be a gentleman, but you can be a councillor right away.

Once convicts were assigned their own wives but now the system is more humane.

All brutes are imperfect animals, man alone is the perfect beast.

GEOGRAPHY

The whole world, except the United States, lies in the temperate zone.

The cold at the North Pole is so great that the towns there are not inhabited.

A Fakir is a Hindu twister.

Oxo is the capital of Norway.

The population of London is a bit too thick.

The wife of Columbus was Columbine.

Persian cats is the chief industry of Persia, hence the word " purr."

Take Ireland, the country where, if it isn't raining bullets on the politicians, it is raining water on the bogs.

If you stand facing north, what have you on your left hand ?   Fingers.

At Cambridge the Thames is called the Cam, but this is only ancient religious prejudice.

The Esquimaux are God's frozen people.

The Irish manyfacksure the following classes of things very exseedingly, namely, linen, bacen, shop eggs and whisky.   The Irish are nearly as fond of bacen as they are of potatoes, and as for whisky, the Irish love it.

The occupations of the Irish people are cattle and vegetables.

What are the main feeders of the Amazon and Orinoco ?   Alligators.

The meridian of Greenwich is a line that isn't there, kept at Greenwich to measure the time with.

The trade of Spain is small, owing to the insolence of the people.

In Holland the people make use of water power to drive their windmills.

The people in Iceland are called Equinoxes.

Australia's rarest inhabitant is the duck-billed platypus. Like all the other inhabitants of Australia, it lays eggs, but unlike them it suckles them.

Asked to name six animals peculiar to the Arctic regions, a boy replied, " Three bears and three seals."

Volcanoes throw out saliva.

A mountain range is a cooking stove used at high altitudes.

There are three kinds of Downs.   North Down, South Down, and Eider Down.

The Menai Straits are crossed by a tubercular bridge.

Switzerland is a very wonderful place, you can often see the mountains touring among the clouds.

The climate of the island is wet but embracing.

Moraines are of two kinds, lateral moraine and maternal moraine.

Crewe is the biggest conjunction in England.

Natal has a very heavy summer rainfall, but most of it falls in the winter.

The chief export of Sheffield is its stainless inhabitants.

How long is Lake Victoria ?   Frifly big.

Sienna is famous for being burnt.

A pass is a low kind of place, very much used, which is natural.

Brussels is famous for its carpets and sprouts.

The horizon is a line where the earth and sky meet, but disappear when you get there.

The sun sets in the west and hurries round to the east to be in time to rise next morning.

The Temperate Zone is the region where no one drinks too much.

The climate of Bombay is such that its inhabitants have to live elsewhere.

The sun never sets on the British Empire because the British Empire is in the East and the sun sets in the west.

Iron is grown in large quantities for manufacturing purposes in South France.

A contour is the outline of a funny shape, such as a broken coastline or a woman.

The probable cause of earthquakes may be attributed to bad drainage and neglect of sewage.

This part of the world is inhabited solely because it is there.

When a volcano has been instinct some time a hard rock stops the chimney up.

The earth is round and flattened at the corners.

What is a cyclone ?   God made them. It sucks.

The winds are dejected because of the rotation of the earth's crust.

In Australia, the grass knows it is a dry climate and so stores up water and is very juicy.

Latitude tells you how hot you are, and longitude how cold you are.

Britain has a temporary climate.

Climate lasts all the time, but weather only a few days.

Volcanoes are due to the infernal heat of the earth.

The three highest mountains in Scotland are Ben Nevis, Ben Lomond, and Ben Jonson.

In a sand storm the camels put their heads in the sand and let the sand find its own destination.

The people of India are divided into casts and outcast.

There is a great deal of nothing in the centre of Australia.

Dresden is the capital of China.

What are warmth producing foods ?   Cayenne pepper and Jamaica ginger, from the countries named.

The river Rhine flows horizontally until it reaches Basle, and then it flows vertically.

Stirling is noted for its fine silver.

People go to Africa to hunt rhinostriches.

Glaciers spread a murrain over the land.

The Australian natives soak the dew into sponges to drink when the water is dry.

The Gulf Stream Drift flows by the British Isles and is even felt so far up as Pittsburg.

Doldrums are a series of high rocks near the Equator. Doldrums are army rum rations.

The chief animals of Australia are the kangaroo, larkspur, boomerang and peccadillo.

The Manchester Ship Canal is very important because before it was made all ships were unloaded at Liverpool and sent by train to Manchester.

Calcutta is at the mouth of the Ganges and is sometimes known as " The Black Hole."

Yeovil is the headquarters of the Surrey Cricket Club.

The three states of water are high water, low water, and break water.

A tableland gets it name from its steep sides and flat top. It's all right when once you are on the top, but it's no joke getting up.

The tides are a fight between the earth and the moon. All water tends towards the moon, because there is no water in the moon, and nature abhors a vacuum. Gravitation at the earth keeps the water rising all the way to the moon. I forget where the sun joins in this fight.

The Arctic regions are neither hot nor cold, they abound in birds of beautiful plumage and of no song such as the elephant and the camel.

Penzance is noted for pirates.

An axis is an imaginary line on which the earth is supposed to take a daily routine.

Name the English lakes.   Ulleswater, Derwent Water, Bayswater, etc.

A blizzard is the inside of a fowl.

The equator is a menagerie line running round the earth and through Africa.

A meridian is the place where they keep the time.

The inhabitants of Paris are called Parisites.

The Plimsoll line is a geographical necessity to prevent sailors getting out of their depth.

The natural regions of Africa are three.   Pasture land, forest land, and Bechuanaland.

Imports are ports very far inland.

Pigmies live in the African forests, and in bad weather they eat frogs and rats, but in fine weather they eat bananas.

Cotton is grown in some parts of the deacon.

A fissure is a man who sells fish.

What shape, roughly, is Scotland ?   It has a lot of arms and legs.

From an essay on irrigation in Egypt.   One of the chief damn places is Aswan.

The Isle of Honolulu is justly celebrated for its climate as well as for its dusky maidens.   Both are praised in current songs.

What is the longest day in the Southern Hemisphere ? Sunday.

The second kind of lakes are those of damned rivers.

From an Oxford School Certificate Geography paper. When next we turn our footsteps towards the Highlands of Scotland or the fjords of Norway, let us remember in contemplating the barrenness of mountains, the highlands of Kenya and repeat the old motto : " It is an ill wind that blows nobody any good."

Although the natives of Hawaii are dark the summers are not oppressive and the winters are not cold.

Define the elements. Mustard, pepper, salt and vinegar.

The earth makes a resolution every twenty-four hours.

Britain is divided into three parts—London, Midland, and Scottish.

An equator is a difficult thing in algebra.

Lions live on the boarders of the desert.

Quinine is the bark of a tree, canine is the bark of a dog.

At Droitwich baths the heaviest people float the highest.

The chief occupation of the inhabitants of Perth is dying.

In France the phesants sleep on mattresses.

The farmers turned their arable land into pasture land, thus making England into a woollen industry.

To irrigate is to disturb.

The modern name of Gaul is vinegar.

Coal is decayed vegetarians.

The Rhine is boarded by wooden mountains.

If 20 feet of an iceberg is above water, the rest is below.

Cecil Rhodes was a great inventor. It was him who invented gold in Africa.

The Tropic of Cancer is where the cancer disease is.

The North Sea is salt because of the Yarmouth bloaters.

The easiest way to cross a range of mountains is to go round them.

England has always been known as a nation of shop-lifters.

Imperial Preference is another name for being presented at Court.

Conway is noted for its turbulent bridge.

The chief bays on the South of England are Torbay, Poole Bay, and Bombay.

The inhabitants of Moscow are called mosquitoes.

The Pyramids are a range of mountains between France and Spain.

The gods of the Indians are chiefly Mahommed and Buddha and in their spare time they do a lot of carving.

A cyclone is a man riding a bicycle.

Black clouds are formed by the evaporation of dirty water.

A volcano is a mountain where the world burst through and the crater is where it spits out.

Much butter is imported from Denmark because cows have greater enterprise and superior technical education than ours.

Reefs are what you put on coffins.

A watershed is where water is kept.

In some rocks there are to be found the fossil footprints of fishes.

Geneva is a beautiful lady, she sometimes rode on a white charger.

Tides are caused by the sun drawing the water out, and the moon drawing it in again.

An isthmus is a bit of land that juts inland.

The Mediterranean and the Red Sea are connected by the sewage canal.

Tributaries of the Nile. Juveniles.

New York stands on the Atlantic sideboard.

In the North of England there is very wet soil and very fertile so that you get good wool and good cotton.

Essay on New Zealand. There is also a great canning industry there.

Its industries are local motives.

The Barren Lands of Canada are mostly desert, and hear are several different fruits such as bananas, figs, cocoanuts, and daits.

From Newport the direction to Ventnor is N.S.S.

Polyps swim about the sea when they are young and when they get old they fasten themselves on their relations and live like that for the rest of their lives.

THE END